# The Red Hat Society and other fragments

Anthony McSherry

Published by Anthony McSherry, 2025.

While every precaution has been taken in the preparation of this book, the publisher assumes no responsibility for errors or omissions, or for damages resulting from the use of the information contained herein.

THE RED HAT SOCIETY AND OTHER FRAGMENTS

**First edition. March 22, 2025.**

Copyright © 2025 Anthony McSherry.

ISBN: 979-8230980971

Written by Anthony McSherry.

To everyone who has taught me

Imagine it, and be thankful it is all there just right *now*, in all its sad and beautiful contingency.

# Introduction

The writing here for me is like the contents of a sketch book where we sketch things down roughly. We can revise and rework and add and do our best to present something interesting, or something that surprises us and is not too tedious for the reader. But for me writing can also become a tedious activity and after a short while the desire to write anything just stops like a well drying up. I need then to be in nature or amongst people, or do ordinary things like paint the garden gate, or so many other things that are miraculous and every day. One could say that writing is just part of that everyday activity also that somehow helps us live. Unfortunately though perhaps, in order to live we have to live in the world, which is not our own. This world includes the 'creations' of others, that is *how* our world has been created through innumerable efforts (of good faith too) by others, conscience and creativity but also innumerable cruelties and mistakes, graspings at reality to form it in our own image. We don't belong anywhere else and that is our problem. We are deeply violent too. We see this more easily as we get older. We can try to change things but those changes themselves become misguided and what they missed becomes part of new revolutions in people's lives. But what they missed does not have to be anything 'good'. What is missed could easily be something 'bad' or evil that we have not recognised or passed over but still remains like a bulb in winter. Some of the sketches here have taken a long time to be gathered together as one's 'here-ness' or place in the world seems often overwhelming even to think about. There are many things I despise that others love. We are all like this. We have to live together like this. The offerings here are sketches, some more polished than others, reflecting the precariousness of trying to understand or describe being here in the world. Some are like internal dialogues, some external with an imaginary other. But they have all been thought about a lot. Many years ago an old friend asked me how I felt. I replied that I felt like a loose tooth. She didn't understand at first. I said I felt like a bird living on one of those sheer cliffs, perched high up on an impossible ledge. Such are perhaps the feelings of being *here* - the 'here-ness' - that provokes me most to sketch anything. It feels as if I am about to come loose or fall and writing steadies me for a while as if my wings will hold.

These sketches also trace out fragments of the becoming involved in practising as a 'talking cure' therapist. It is through this lens as a counsellor and psychotherapist that I write most of these sketches as that work has come to mean so much to me. If I had become a carpenter I would be writing in a different way. They seem to have been created through a side-effect of being with others in therapy but reflect a life almost lived (in the sense of not fully lived as fulfilling one's potential and also as one coming to its end). In a previous short book, it seemed like sketches like this were a random collection of thoughts that begin to show a pattern reflecting the collector (see *On Friendship*), and this is also the case here although both collections are loose. I have found that we cannot take ourselves out of the picture even if we make an effort not to be in it, like taking a photograph. The photographer is always there. As I said before, we try to express *ourselves* in whatever we do, be it the conscientious litter picker or the vain quantum physicist. So, here in order not to lie to you the reader I am probably just doing that, expressing my *self* whatever that is. Sketching the self. You could say that perhaps all of life's work in its entirety for all of us is a self-portrait. It is a strange experience to even try as often what comes out is a vanity in oneself simply in being oneself. I don't like such narcissism but have not avoided it often.

The title was going to be, *On Freedom*, linked to aspiring to something which perhaps we all want but cannot describe or know properly. However, I changed it to *The Red Hat Society* to see this from another angle. Amongst vague notions of wanting to be very wealthy and 'successful' (whatever that means) other notions hold a stronger sway over perhaps many of us when we think of freedom.

What comes to mind for me are the hours as a child spent staring up at the stars in our exiled garden, away from the chaos, as if slowly being absorbed into the starry universe with its huge empty spaces which nevertheless offered an imaginary welcome and recognition. But the universe must be *indifferent* to us of course. We hear on television programs now that we are all just stardust but there was a longing on that childhood garden wall to be more than that. Are we not all like this in some way? It is a longing which still insists even given the indifferences of some distant galaxy or point of light. We should not even assign such a personal attribute to the universe. It is only people who are indifferent to each other. The universe is beyond such things. A different register of species. But still looking up at the stars, the cold ridge of the capstones pressing into my back, there was something about a notion of 'being free' which I couldn't and still don't quite understand. It vaguely has something to do with not being caught up in what others demand and so being free of *people* in some important way. The privacy of our lives however is always counterintuitively held in place by the publicity of our lives also. It is why lovers grow tired of each other, and recognisable achievements become dead to the touch. We seem to be held in some balance, some oscillating space between the private and the public that is essential to our wellbeing. If either space claims a hegemony it becomes corrupt or toxic and we enter into a despair which at first may be unnoticeable. Thus the despair of even the best dictatorships whether public or private. This is a sketch book then noting that oscillation of despair of being in this world, a kind of wrestling match that we all have to win, even up to the very moment of a defeat. If some of the writing here looks like a poem it certainly is not meant to be. Spaces and line endings are more about pauses to breathe and think, or for the effect of space than any metre or rhyme. Many of these sketches need to be read aloud or even acted as if on stage.

Any characters portrayed in this collection are fictional, with any resemblance to actual people purely accidental, including sketches which appear like fragments of case studies.

### What are you trying to be free of?

Many people come to therapy because they want to be free of something although that might not be clear initially. Freedom is such a vague idea that it cannot be defined like a technical term. But what comes to mind for me are different levels of freedom. The basic level is not being compelled to live as something like a feudal serf, a slave of any kind, or an indentured servant. We could ask ourselves also whether mortgages (and all debt) are a form of slavery or indenture. Surely everything associated with them must be. Surely each person ought to have a right to a secure shelter that is worthy of being called 'home'? What kind of vile societies are we living in that we cannot yet affirm this basic idea without it being linked to humiliation of some kind?

The next level is not being compelled to comply with any dominant discourse of oppression, such as a political view, a religious view, or any tradition that oppresses. You will find these kinds of freedoms in Human Rights legislation. We could put capitalism under the heading of an oppressive world view also - we have to if not just to keep open the possibility that it is not a 'natural' way to function.

The third level of freedom and that which this writing is about must refer to the *intra-psychical* and *relational* freedoms both of which are inextricably interlinked. These latter two interlinked freedoms are closely related to one's social and family history. That is what I think of when I think of one's 'history'. But one's history must be linked to the other two levels also of security and freedom from oppression. They must be immersed in each other and so to separate them is artificial to an extent.

Psychotherapy is not the only way but it is one way of freeing oneself from one's history. It's not about social revolution although it could lead to that indirectly. We could envisage that in some cases psychotherapy could *only* be about social revolution because to live in an entirely crushing regime or situation could also crush the spirit so much that it is not worth living at all. There are plenty of examples.

But why would anyone want to be free of their history? Most people do not as they don't see a problem. Family portraits abound. Flags fly. Bands march. The question does not occur to them. In fact, they want to entrench their history even more as it makes them feel safe and have a sense of belonging. The problems they see are 'outside' in others, or in others' histories. They might even be right sometimes. We will leave the entrenched in their dugouts.

The only reason we would want to be free of our history would be to relieve or change an intra-psychical distress or a relational distress which that history is creating. We might want to change the past, or more realistically understand it differently which changes it in an important sense. You could say we no longer want to be who we were and want to become who we ought to be or aspire to be instead. But can it be that simple? Because if you look at your life from an imaginary height there may have been times in it when you were being in a way that seemed the best possible way at least for a while even though this vision of oneself then disappears into a drudgery, a form of enslavement you could say, or the dullness of being, or worse, some horror of living such as living in bad faith. So one's life can be viewed as a flickering of ways of being that appeared good or bad or somewhere in between, sometimes especially brilliant or shining and at others (probably the most part) a kind of lack of light altogether. We would surely want to be free of this lack of light if we think of light as enlightening. But it could be that the dimmest of light at points in your life was a signal of the best part but was outshone by the brightness of other events, false trails, false hopes and false dreams.

We only know some things through the *experience* of these. Such a thing that only comes from experience and not thought is often a tragedy. There will be elements of our lives that can't quite be understood without tipping into some abyss. We find those parts by accident. At best they leave us knowing we cannot see something clearly, knowing what that something might be only indistinctly like a shape in the fog, that we cannot walk there. Others will be able to see it although we might not accept they can. And there will be elements which we thought would destroy us on understanding but didn't at all and set us free. Being able to think clearly is so important here and also the capacity to trust one's thoughts. How do we learn to trust our own thinking?

Returning to the first two levels, the path and the price of going looking to free oneself is disillusionment with those human projects of nationalism, egotism, vanity, wealth, and prestige in the eyes of others. There are other things to add here also. But it is a lonely path with few companions along the way.

So the question as to what are you trying to be free of is crucial. It seems to me that it cannot be answered easily on a personal level at all. We have to find from experience what it is we want to be freed from and that is a problem.

## What we ask of the client and ourselves

When you hear seagulls where does it take you?

(carnivorous beak, merciless eye)

The old canal basin feeding the ducks

(two masseuses on a smoke break, a breast carelessly exposed)

The scent of rust on wrought iron railings

(piss smells by the urinals)

Endless sunny Victorian promenades

(broken pavements where you could split your head open)

Shining fields where someone said seagulls come in to shelter before a storm

(Keep Off. Private Land)

But most of all I think of ocean cliffs and big skies that welcome you as you are

(And so on).

## High babies (or being held by the other)

There is a photograph of me as a child. About 5 or 6. It must be high babies. My hands are resting one over the other in front of me at a small wooden desk. Letters of the alphabet behind on the wall in capitals and lower case, each a kind of restrained swirl as if preparing for longhand. They must have been in colour. My hands are small and soft, creased and curved as if some artist has tried to make something perfect. My jumper is a soft white or maybe cream or a very light yellow. It is soft wool and I think my mother knit it. I am looking directly at the camera with that unselfconscious look of young children, like an animal would look. I am slightly squinting. Some perplexity at being photographed, at the words of the photographer. I wish I could remember the photographer. But he is lost in time to me. He was a man I am sure. But I may have imagined him. He will be wearing a brown suit from the mid-1960s, with those flares, and long collars. His hands will be white and almost bony, fingers long and crooked at the joints like twigs. He is imagined. I am looking at him in perplexity. My unknown companion who will never be there who I continually look out at now from the photographic paper for as long as eternity or the paper last.

Neither of us is important now, except to you dear imagined reader for a few moments. I am looking out into the future that is you unknown to me.

But let me tell you a few things. I was in love with a nun in high babies.

## A funeral (or being held by the other)

We were teenagers too once in the shaded yew walk of the 1970s, the small gravestones hidden in the dry ground of a clearing. Us boys lining the path in silence, the solemn procession and the swish of priests' vestments. Patrick Kavanagh was the favourite of our English teacher whose funeral it was. I can still hear that gravelly voice like a brook. But clagging over dull boulder clay trying to polish the rough stones that we were. In that glacial drift of religion too there was too much roughness and muck for him. He should have shaken it off - along with all that priestly nonsense and set himself free. Go write love poems like his hero. Dear God!

"Fly off and do your own thing!" I would have said to him if I'd been his Dad I tell you. "Get out and live! God is dead! Set yourself free!" That's what I would have said.

Why did I feel so close to this stranger there in the Yew walk? In class once he picked me up on my spelling. It was the word 'umbrella'.

"You're spelling is off," he proclaimed as if it were something rancid. He announced my surname like it was a bit of that clay he couldn't shake off as well.

"How do you *say* it? How do you *say* 'umbrella'?" he asked and showed me how in one go. Holding too tightly to my essay book between his fingers and his thumbs as if to keep himself in the world.

Embarrassed and not used to such questioning, I carefully pronounced the word as the class looked on in silence.

um

beh

reh

la.

That is how we said it in Dublin. He caught my look and softened in some way for he was not a cruel man. He tapped out the correct spelling on the board, ignoring the chalk stick crumbling in his shaking hand.

At his funeral we stood in dumb curiosity like thoughtless calves as if death could never approach our endless vitality.

Six of the biggest boys carried his coffin. One was in tears.

Not with grief but the weight of it.

## Given

The given is when we start saying to ourselves "Am I being congruent now?" Or "Why is it hard to be empathic here?" Or "Why do I need to keep this person at a distance?" Or "I must learn to understand this counter-transference", or "Keep the boundaries steady..." In these instructions and questions, and in the terminology, there is a dead repository of given knowledge - dead does not mean it is not helpful - and also too there is a hint of the sensual that has not yet shown itself. The presence of the sensual in these dead phrases, in the questioning and instructions, can be found in the body - in oneself. In *you* yourself. As if those phrases are inflected by the body, the body of memory - oneself - in a way that speaks something that can't be found in the words themselves. We might even after a while come to realise that in the questions we ask ourselves, and in the language of the client, there is coming forward a delight in violence to the other - and the sensuality reveals itself much like a carnivore moving and disguising its way through foliage. And it might be something the client - or the therapist - is unaware of in themselves: they might think they are in fact the gentlest of souls and the strange anxiety they feel is because other people are so stupid or violent. Or it could be many other things.

This gives the lie to 'authenticity' - it isn't that in order to be authentic we have to give full flight to the carnivorous violence. That we have to 'express ourselves'. But neither must we fly from it (Ask yourself from where comes the word 'must' here). We have to know who we are and decide carefully how to live or proceed insofar as we can (Where does 'have to' come from here?), or insofar that it is possible to do so at all.

Some people I find I have to give up on.

## The benefits of disappointment

It's well known that the child's consciousness of love has to shift away from the parents so much so that parental love exists in another world that cannot reach them any longer apart from care in crises. The child's existential need is directed outwards towards some 'other' love. This is the loss involved in parenthood. Your child must move into another realm in order to live even if they may physically live next door.

You must let them go though it be through hell or high water.

Yet it seems to me that they are always looking back too. Looking back to a lost love that they would wish to find most ardently. A love of the father, a love of the mother - whichever one was lacking the most or was once the most ardent and unfulfilled, looking back as if for it to be fulfilled, as if it could ever be fulfilled. This road always leads to disappointment, as does the other road.

But I'm not sure if many people reach the full benefits and fruition of such disappointments and instead there is a holding on to some dream of love - of a love that will come towards us, *for us*, holding us and recognising us in an ardent acceptance. The journey across the gravity fields and empty spaces of these emotions, relations, and interactions with others are *lifetime* journeys whether we like them or not. They are the fabric of life. It is difficult to traverse them alone, without having had a mentor, or a companion of the psyche, who can respect what you found.

## Dialogue on a pebble

"Finally disentangled, in some shaded vision from your weight, having crawled out I'm out forever. Unsteady, wet, like a newborn calf slapped into life. But the effort of it is mine and no-one else's, you must declare truthfully. Although others have set me steady on my feet I have had to take the steps *alone* out of your atmosphere, your gravitational field, this *thing* we were."

"You're not talking about me. Are you?"

"No. I'm glad you're here."

"You mean to say this thing is now a starry ornament, a star collapsed upon itself, its atmosphere blown away at last in the crush. Like you can put it in your pocket like a pebble. You mean to say that something that was most important to you is like a pebble now, held easily in a small hand, a small rough diamond and the important person won't know it now but that will have to be all right."

"Sadly yes it's what I mean to say. But I was misled. I misled myself."

"You've changed your mind?"

"Yes. I think now that we are always in relation to others no matter how far they are from our lives as we live every day from day to day. We just imagine or feel that we are in control of everything like having a pebble in our pocket. Some of us might well *have to* imagine that as otherwise it is too difficult. But if we keep imagining being in control and believing we are *right* then we are just like politicians or generals smiling and shaking hands after ordering an atrocity."

"That is how they can bear..."

"Bear the atrocity yes."

"So experience is misleading."

"If not called to give an account of itself."

"There is something at the start about being disentangled that I like."

## Exposure

When people talk about the meaning of psychotherapy they often talk about self-awareness, acceptance and understanding. In short, about knowledge of oneself. We can divide knowledge into given meanings and sensual meanings, the former widely circulating and the latter private (of the personal life of the person, even of the unknown or unconscious). But beyond knowledge what is psychotherapy about? Is it possible even to speak of or write of what is beyond knowledge? Is that a question that is even valid to ask? The beyond of knowledge is something that we cannot know surely.

We always appear to *want* something. And just as in life we are always after something in therapy. Some prize whose guise is often knowledge. And so it's astonishing to meet those who come to therapy to explore their lives and ways of living rather than trying to grasp at that particular prize. They want a *different* prize. They see already that knowledge is always only a byproduct like an unfortunate pollutant. Love is the real thing for them.

Maybe I could rephrase that. Love is the activity of psychotherapy that we are interested in (which may be embarrassing to admit). Knowledge is only its byproduct, one which we become addicted to and pretend is the most important thing. Like sugar, or caffeine, or alcohol. People become bloated on it and full of themselves. So, if we agree that knowledge is just the byproduct would that mean that love is its product? No. Love is its activity. Perhaps this is why so many cannot bear it. And we are astonished at those who can. This kind of love also shows us how we affect others.

This is such an unusual space that very few people want to enter it. Some are incapable of entering it. Many wouldn't bother with it as they see no profit in it. I often think anyone who stays has been exposed to its activity by accident. So what then is the product of psychotherapy? It must be a kind of self-love that is non-narcissistic. That helps us see that self-acceptance is a form of knowledge but is also a form of activity that calls us to account. If someone is a danger to others then self-acceptance only helps if it is accompanied by a process of calling to account which changes the self.

And what is this activity or process? We cannot simply be told something that makes us better. We have to feel that what is being communicated has real importance to the other person involved. There is an activity that shows that the therapist's own being is affected by what is being opened up in the relation with you. It seems fair to call this realness love. The messages that go to and fro have to be received and given in love. It is as if love is the flour without which nothing will hold together.

## Love's force

My own existentialism. Is there such a thing? Yes, of course. We're all existentialists since we all exist. I suppose mine is not only a Sartrean one because his is a bleak 'no' to life (although his generosity is not). I say this even though as it struck Sartre so it strikes everyone who looks properly at life harshly and without mercy that we are contingent and in this there is a tragedy and a freedom. I am free to take my own life if I wish, or embrace with a martyr's gusto a lifetime of suffering. Even in the dingiest prison I am free. But my own 'yes' to life has a resemblance to the attitude of Camus or Molly Bloom. The earth is our home for a short while between eternities of non-existence, where we can let the ocean's salt and the sun's warmth glisten on us, even by perfumed gardens. A 'yes' to our existence in a kind of leap of faith. If we want to live non-narcissistically this attitude must permeate how we think of the other person, impossible though it is at times. The other is the same although they might not know it or feel it. Because they are the same does not mean you will ever know them however and this is crucial. We have to nurture their own act of faith, a non-narcissistic leap towards becoming, and that is existentialism too.

Someone I know once asked a melancholic suicidal woman, "Why are you in such a hurry? - we'll all be dead in thirty years or so anyway. Do you think you're eternal or something and your suffering will be forever?" Somehow in the way my acquaintance said it there was an activity that propelled the logic into something real and alive which relieved her of her narcissism. She was the same as each of us and this set her free to be for others and herself once again. But such an affect only took place through an activity of love that propelled the logic to create a home or receptivity in her. That activity is the mystery.

## Existential becoming

I wonder is it only in the most difficult times are we called into existence. The person who has had an easy life may not exist then technically. Does such a person exist? Hard to think that if you have had an easy life you may not exist.

## Innocent

One of the most important things that ever happened to me was one night when my baby was still a very young baby. A few months at most. About 3am she had needed a bottle. I sat quietly with her in my boxers and T shirt, tiredness draped around me like an old shawl. The bottle had been put aside but she stayed awake. I looked carefully at her face, into her eyes, and this expression begins to spread across her face. What was it? Her little gummy mouth contorted then formed into a smile as delicate as a rose petal. I smiled back. Our eyes holding each other's gaze in some everlasting promise. The promise came from me. The trust from her.

Is it possible to call such a bond anything else but a loving one? Can we be cynical and call it a loving narcissistic bond? Or even only a narcissistic bond? To these last two questions the answer is affirmative *only* if we go on to provoke in our child the belief that others are not of moral value in the world. So it is the narcissistic damage in the adult (if it is there) that is mirrored back to the child that will become the problem. The infant is always an innocent.

## Listening

Active listening can mislead. There is so much in it that is dead.

You have to stay alive instead to something else soaked in words as it is in the torrent. Follow those words that glitter with life over the weirs and mill races keeping sight of them in the flood.

You are a fish flying and diving with them.

## The difference

From the very beginning I thought that the therapeutic was ontological. We *become* therapeutic rather than behaving as if we are, or having clever answers or behaving therapeutically in some given fashion. The ontological is to provoke in oneself the being-oneself that is therapeutic like nurturing a wild garden where weeds grow alongside everything else rather than a manicured space. Eventually there are no such things as weeds. This is a life's work rather than learning a 'skill set'. It is crucial to know the difference between life-work and skill. That doesn't mean that we don't need to think knowledgeably and critically.

**Going beyond** (**or a fragment of an interior dialogue with a supervisor**)

In therapy there are so many things in play.

"She needs me to acknowledge her sexuality and her beauty but not *accuse* her for it, to accept and regard her for who she is rather than what desires she can provoke in the other and how that might make *you* feel."

"But this has to be real."

"Yes of course. She knows she provokes these desires and she knows that I look past and through them, but *along* with them don't forget, towards someone else."

"Provokes?"

"Well, I mean she is attractive but also there is some need in her, or something, that wants to fascinate."

"Are we not all like that at some level though? We want to be interesting."

"Yes. We want to be interesting for others at some level."

"There's a thin line between that and being degraded I think often."

"Sure. For sure. There is a whole world and worlds of acknowledgement here as the other as desiring of her as not degrading, as acknowledging the attraction of degradation even also, but walking along with this towards a different experience of herself as maybe curious, funny, and cared about in the sense of minded, kept in mind, and *far beyond me*."

"There is so much more here. For example, can you allow someone to be *far beyond you*?"

"I think I can."

"Well that's how you work. How you are."

"But to open a pathway for her to go far beyond me is what counts."

"That is what always counts. Letting the other go far beyond us. We're always bloody hampering people."

## On death

Judging from how we live some people will look back at their life from their death bed and judge it as a success based on the things they got. The material things. So let's imagine when they get to heaven and meet their old friends, will they ask, "What did you *get*? How *much* did you get?"

Can you imagine a heaven like that? Would it make any sense? Yet when humans meet old friends by accident this is how they often behave. In an interior dialogue they will say to themselves "I'm glad I was wearing that expensive new coat." Are you one of those 'some people'? And it just goes to show there's no heaven at all also.

## The truth

The truth comes through a million prisms that are forever shifting. Some prismatic truths return like insistent memories.

We hold onto these returns as if they say something crucial about ourselves we could never let go of. But once we say them they shift. It's like trying to grasp the light shattering on a puddle.

Truth is never arrived at through a logical process but through the senses, a life lived, or by accident. It hits you in the chest like an anxiety. Freud's free association stumbles into something by *accident* (that is its outcome if left to itself).

That is not to say that we always say the truth by accident.

And we always want to address the truth to someone who can no longer hear it.

The truth is always to be continued.

## Not broken… just injured

Still half dark in the garden. Light rain on the muddy field of wakening just before sunrise breaks out. Look at the pegs on the line they are like notes waiting to be written. The sun shade will have to pass for an umbrella. A blackbird is tuning up filling the air in someone else's garden over past those big fir trees that someone cut half down. Seems like much further away than it is. The rain is beginning to insist.

But undeterred he's all of a sudden near me singing his blackbird music. Everything is held together in his quivering throat until a crow passing through breaks in all out of tune. Then both are gone. Everything falls apart. Disappointment spreads like the rain. Only moments have passed but it could have been a lifetime. I hope the cat is in or too tired from its night time sport to bother about the stupid game of killing.

In the shed there is a bird I rescued. Some feathers are missing from his neck where the cat got him. An almost cartoon bite shape showing where the killer just missed. Worse is the damaged wing. Hopefully not broken but just injured. A quite beautiful pigeon. Amber eyes. Feathers iridescent greens and blues against the greys, and then those wing tips like the white wings of jets. Acrobat and jet of the sky.

I'll fast forward for you now. He *did* recover. As if by slow magic feathers grew back and the wing realigned. Then one morning after one of our tests with what seemed like enormous force he took flight, his wings catching the heavy summer air as if almost sure to break. But break they did not. He circled and swooped between the cut-down trees then gained height. I thought he was still injured but he was just taking his bearings before he shot off like an arrow.

"Go!" I wanted to shout, "and never come back!" but the clap of his wings returned the thought to me. He didn't need it. Incomprehensible to each other all the way from his rescue to his recovery and flight. Not knowing I was his saviour I followed his arc over the high trees towards the open fields not knowing that he had become mine.

## Fooling ourselves

"Can bad faith be repaired?"

No. It can only not be repeated. The distance between the decision of bad faith and learning to live with its consequences can be a lifetime.

"So try to get it right first time. Know yourself. But that's impossible. How to deal with the impossibility?"

For most people the desire for money overrides any considerations of bad faith. Financial 'success' is the great universal salve for a wounded conscience. They think they know themselves through money.

"So the impossible is made possible through another act of bad faith? Trusting in the salve of money."

Yes, at least I think so. But even if you could do the impossible, if you could truly repair an act of bad faith or always act in good faith then what? Then you might be fooled by other circumstances, in all innocence.

"What kind of other circumstances?"

I can think of two. We fool ourselves in good faith, and we are deceptive to others. So these two are traps along the way.

"What would be fooling ourselves in good faith?"

An example would be getting carried away by our desires, thinking they are good for us and so must be good in general, or good for *you*. Or naivety.

"I see that."

And an example of deception is that we convince another that they need something which they do not.

"I see that. I can think of a lot of examples of deception."

We are the great deceivers, aren't we? It is in the distance between being fooled, being deceived and acceptance of such inevitability that a whole life's wisdom might unfold.

"This sounds like a sad state of affairs. Is there no other way?"

Unthinking custom, ritual and tradition gets us off the hook. But excludes thinking for yourself and excludes others.

"How does it exclude others?"

Try walking into a church or something like that and saying you are a non-believer. You'll see then. Or better still, try leaving a church after you have walked into one.

"I might try."

But still the tragedy of many people's lives is that they have no tradition in which to frame their lives to get them off the hook. They are left instead to the ravages of the world and a freedom that is beyond their ability to cope with. But the tragedy for many is just such a tradition.

"And what are we left with then?"

But you must know already.

"Ah, yes, we are left with just ourselves."

A 'just ourselves' that is not excluding. That is our new tradition.

"I might give it a try."

After this dialogue there was a long silence. After the long silence the speaker who was not so full of himself said almost to himself, "Maybe we should just leave others alone, and stop interfering all the time in other people's lives, stop thinking we know best, as long as no-one gets abused or murdered."

## The musician

The hermit decided never to look at the beauty of the world again. He saw it as a better place to be to be above the world. But of course it was his vanity that drew him there to that place high up in the mountains. So as not to be subject to the beauty of the world. In his vanity he had cut himself off from it, thinking he was contemplating something better, eternal beauty, instead. A beauty more worthy *of himself.*

It would have been better for him if he'd stayed down in the valley, like that musician, desperately trying to win that girl's attention.

## People's faces

When you read people's faces, in their coming and going, everyday activities, there is always a kind of worry. In the bright bubbling life of the teenager, and the candid optimist, there is the always present sense of our own end, the contingent and unnecessary centrality of ourselves. Death itself - not just an abstract form or idea - the ultimate means of our non-recognition, the everlasting non-possibility of meeting the smile of the other, or the friendly word (or you could say the whole sensual world).

You will find this worry there. It sometimes paralyses me into an endless non-decision.

## Self-possession

If you can't find a dignity in your own self that is worth fighting for then don't try to find that dignity in others - as you will have left behind what is most important about *you,* your own experience of yourself. You mustn't leave this behind. It will come back to haunt you at every step if you do.

This is an idea that comes through the experience of self-possession, of being in possession of one's own self (which doesn't mean that you cannot find yourself through others). We cannot define self-possession but know it is something real. It can be felt in the experience of falling asleep. Or felt in the experience of understanding a problem. And in many other experiences. It is not a trance or mindfulness.

You could ask then what is the dignity of your own self? It could be the self-possession not to be humiliated even just as life or someone tries to humiliate you. So self-possession involves, silence, inaction, speech and action.

## Keepers of secrets

Most of us have a prior history of keeping secrets for others. It comes 'naturally' in this sense for therapists to do so in their work. We don't disclose names or places of work. We try to protect the identity of the other person in every way possible as if locked away in some vault.

What is troublesome is having to keep a secret that you did not want to be entrusted with. This kind of secret is an unwelcome burden and it could break a friendship in the sense that you become a therapist for the other and no longer a friend. If you wish to keep a friend, don't imprison them with too heavy a secret. How to weigh how heavy a secret is may be impossible however.

Yet, let's assume your friend is educated and polite, even thoughtful. Would you ever say 'no' to such a friend who wanted to share with you a secret? Even if you knew the secret itself would devastate you. This is the predicament we should never put another person in. And on a lesser level, if a friend shares a secret let them tell you it is a secret and not presume you know that. Because to you it might be nothing at all.

There is that irreplaceable bond, its irreplaceable value, of the other knowing us in our deepest abjection and still offering us that loving space of acceptance, privacy, acknowledgement, and openness to understanding. This is the highly valuable and enduring space between two people. Perhaps only someone like a therapist can be this kind of keeper of secrets. Not a friend.

## Use/no use

Survival over ethics is the ethics of our day. The ethics of individualism within capitalism. Success equates to money. A false ethics. Some would say no real ethics at all.

The question facing especially children and young people is what 'use' they are to this world of the ethics of generating money. It might not be a question they fully understand yet but it places them in a situation of having to think of selling *themselves* in some way – their precious time, their energy, the activity of their minds and bodies. In a capitalist system it is easy for young people to feel that they have no *intrinsic* value that would enable them to live in a world that assigns a low value to being a person. It's almost easy to fool yourself on this if you live in Western Europe where people may have more rights than in other places.

But if you are of no use to helping the capitalist to 'get on' – to fulfilling his 'instructions' handed down by others who are a product of the system, to prosper financially in the world - then you will be discarded in some shape or form. This ideology flows underneath Western 'rights' like a long-forgotten drainage system. The idea of each of us having a responsibility towards the dignity of others has not taken hold and seems absurd if you dig beneath a little. The dignity of the other and of oneself has to be enforced to a minimal degree by law, which just goes to show it's not intrinsic to us at all.

You could ask yourself what laws you *really* follow in life. What underflowing drainage system irrigates your roots?

I read once in a popular financial section of a paper about 'juicy' funds. The word brought up images of food, meat cooked rarely, choice cuts of only the best, laden tables and fat bellies. Gluttony. Greed. But also of the existential need for food. Our existence depends on it. The need for wealth, to control the resources of food and shelter, and for the weak to be 'of use' in order to have access to adequate wealth, seems to be the ground of all our prestige.

As my grandmother said, "when hunger comes in the door love goes out the window." And as someone else said, "Better to be an old man's darling than a young man's slave."

We have to do better than this surely?

## A thought on types of thinking

Visualise this. Imagine a series of three dimensional waves intersecting and overlapping - the three dimensional space is 'covered' through a wave-like texture of meanings that interlink and overlap. This is like analogue thinking, in waves not particles. There are no gaps but meanings present themselves as waves and interference in a three dimensional fabric (which brings its own problems). It can be found in the word 'analogy'*.

Now imagine instead a three dimensional network of many rigid wire meshes overlapping - the gaps between are easily seen, and these are the gaps where 'analogue' context would have been. It takes a longer and more analytical process to understand what the gaps indicate or may invite us to think about, almost through a process of three-dimensional integration homing in on an infinitesimal difference (but one which could be crucial). 'Context' is not there but has to be 'homed in' on. This is the logic of thinking more prevalent in the 'neurodiverse' world (which presents its own problems).

In the analogue world we say it is 'like' this... and we make a comparison or analogy or many of them. The 'like' here contains a myriad of wave forms overlapping and we cannot explain how we know their meaning clearly. It seems to be that through an overlapping of numerous analogies the meanings simply 'appear' like magic.

In the concrete world of particles (or three dimensional straight lines of the wire mesh) we have to say 'I have not seen this particle before so I do not know it' but it 'reminds me' of this particle or that straight line. The 'reminder' may be out of context because there is no easy path at first to the right context. The meaning has to be deduced through a process of rigid logic that itself can go astray.

We can't but see the beauty in both ways. There must be other ways too.

*owed to Sally Parsloe

## The Gardens of Sallust

The class element in psychotherapy. For a few years I used to go for supervision in a posh part of London. Up at all hours. The house was one of those lovely Georgian buildings with a huge glossy front door, the stained glass above it fanned out like a peacock's tail. A chandelier in the hallway reminded me of a tenement we lived in as children. But far from a tenement this one was. I was ushered into a large room with brand new bespoke bookshelves filled with books. Two armchairs, paintings on the walls, a bare fireplace, a writing desk and rich cream Roman blinds. Persian rugs, a cream sofa, a silver standard lamp. I faced the window and the supervisor would lower the blinds to shade my eyes from the rising sun as we met so early to fit me in.

A despondent thought caught hold of me one bleak winter morning. It takes a certain kind of manic dedication for someone with little money to embark on a training as an analyst or a psychotherapist (who is required to go to long-term therapy and endless supervision). They will have to abandon all hopes of owning property, or having children, at least for a good or a bad many years unless someone is there to subsidise it all. Or you are willing to live as poor as a church mouse. It takes far less sacrifice for someone with the available money in some form. This class element carries the poison of snobbery, condescension and disgust. Knowledge and the power it brings become 'class-ified'. Perhaps there are the 'self-made' who will deny all of this and tell me to get the chip off my shoulder.

Even so, that winter morning when our meeting was even earlier than usual I *was* the *poveraccio*. An object of pity given a cup of tea (never to be repeated). The poor supervisor wasn't to know that I thought I was Francis of Assisi in the Gardens of Sallust.

I wish her no harm. But I can understand the Bolsheviks.

## An address to the unknown you

If you ever get up early not having slept great on a clear morning while it's still dark go out into the garden or onto the balcony, or onto the street and look up at the sky. Out there you'll find the stark indifferent beauty of the universe colder than ice doing its thing. It took someone like Newton to catch a predictability in it: Everything stays in place until something is knocked out of place into some endless trajectory and how gravity fields hold everything steady as if it is in place forever.

"That sounds a bit like us."

But looking up at the stars you get that other sense that our tragedy is that we cease to know the world, that we end.

"What freedom is there in knowing such a thing?"

You could count three kinds of knowing here. The first is that mathematical Newtonian kind which I barely understand although many others do.

"Still how long did it take for a second Newton to come along?"

The second is the phenomenal knowing of the whole sensual world on which you depend. You were built for gravity and you are protected by magnetic fields you cannot even feel. But you were built for something else too. Others, the world and the universe are present to you through the phenomenal reality of the senses and their memory which you cannot often feel either.

"I get that."

The third kind of knowing is that tragic one, that we know our own end is inevitable, that we cease and return to the material, susceptible to the mathematical, the quantifiable. They could weigh your ashes.

"I bet they do."

And this infinity of the soul we feel is just a temporary state of mind that will cease and take all its inexpressible beauty with it. I mean only our body makes it happen. We know this third kind of knowing through language just like we know a sentence ends and we feel alive as long the sentence continues to speak itself. We never wish for the writing and the speaking to end and it is always addressed to someone, someone 'out there', to *you*. The same goes with music, art, speech and everything else. And you must respond. When we are with another person these fields of knowledge intersect and we begin to understand that living knowledge as being. If there is not an intersection of living knowledge fields, of 'living-ness', we feel dead. This is why friendship and all sorts of other relationships can be so difficult. Because our gravity fields don't intersect.

"Did you mean *me* just now?"

I always mean you. Everything I say is for you.

## Death as change

Autumn leaves suddenly become something real, as if for the first time they have been noticed. In their colours a reminder of what seems most implicit in therapy as the relation to death. We could say change and death. The brightness of the leaves, the multiplicity of shades speaking of change. If we do not let something die, nothing new can be born. If we cannot change then we have to accept not changing. In this way, death inhabits and skirts every life.

## Death as contingency

Imagine this moment in the twilight without the sound of a person you love preparing dinner. It doesn't have to be a lover or a partner of some kind - try to get out of that dull mindset. In fact, specifically don't let it be a lover - in order to set yourself free of it. Imagine it without the familiar stillness of the garden, without the cat still as a statue by your chair. Imagine it, and be thankful it is all there just right *now*, in all its sad and beautiful contingency. See the cat has already moved away. Death as contingency inhabits every step.

## Death as indecision

When you read people's faces in their coming and going and everyday activities there is always the shadow of some kind of worry. Even in the bright bubbling life of the teenager and the candid optimist there is the always present sense of our own end, the contingent and unnecessary centrality of ourselves. Death itself as an abstract form and idea. Only until it becomes real, and then you're gone. We are fully material only in death. The ultimate means of our non-recognition, the everlasting non-possibility of meeting the smile of the other, or the friendly word, or its violence and indifference (or you could say the whole sensual human world).

You will find this in faces over there, here, everywhere. It sometimes paralyses you into an endless non-decision, a never-ending false stability.

## Loss and freedom

Some women are trapped inside their own beauty. Trapped but unable to push open the unlocked gate. And the same goes for some men. The same goes for ugliness. And we who were once free become trapped with them. Break free I'm telling you! Break free! These words crossed my mind the first time I met this woman. And they may well have been addressed to myself as much as to everyone else. Where they came from or what they meant I wasn't sure of.

Working with someone who is beautiful is the most distracting of things. It is like working with someone who is in love but in the case of beauty it is the therapist who stops being able to think. If beauty traps us in a kind of enchantment we know too that enchantments end and something different has to show itself for us to live. I would call this something different an eternal beauty in the other person (and in ourselves) which finally they (and we) come into contact with or which they (and we) begin finally to take seriously. Even though such personal eternity is bound by the finiteness of our living bodies.

She had just quit her job as a lap dancer. Like all women she knew who found themselves earning money this way she hated men with an energy that permeated every word and action. But she was aware of it and tried to think about it carefully unlike a lot of those other women who pandered to certain men or feared them. She hated men for how they looked at her, hated men for how she had power over them and hated men for how they hated her for having that power. And most of all perhaps she hated men for needing them. There seemed to be no way out of it. She told me all of this matter-of-factly like reading from a script. But some of her words stood out like signposts in a grim landscape.

"A lot of them are married. I see them collecting their kids at school, going shopping with the wife, most of them don't recognise me in real life."

Her words threw me into a kind of dreamworld and I wondered which was real life for her former customers. Their 'real life' or their visits to the lap dancing club? Call them clients and I wondered where lap dancing and therapy coincided. Therapy is such a strange space that it could be said to be not real at all, as it often seems like a dream space where strange creatures of the psyche come forward like circus performers. But in a way it is more real than real life as the endless circus of one's psyche shows itself in all its regalia and tightrope anxieties. Memories of my own therapies showed such a circus where some things were 'real-ised' forever, changing the imaginary characters, the characters that can now move again, surprise us again and speak or even sing. Although we haven't met for many years I still love my therapists like old (not always Platonic) lovers or friends who we no longer see and with whom I still have impassioned arguments and rows in my mind. The love in therapy is a strange love, an abstinent love that is as real as any other. I would never know if any of them missed *me* in such a way. I may well be forgotten completely, just some shadow of a memory or nothing like what I can imagine. In this dreamworld in the room with this client I wondered why thoughts of love and being forgotten about were there like lost ghosts moving between us.

In our sessions she always wore loose casual clothes which unintentionally perhaps accented rather than disguised her shape. No makeup. Her hair seemed to flow without much care over her shoulders. Another signpost.

"Yes, it's not dyed," catching my look as if catching a ball that was heading out of bounds.

I smiled in a kind of surrender. Yes she would know any traces of sexual desire directed towards her or any curiosity about her physical self. 'All men were predators, you are a man therefore you are a predator' was the logic. I thought of the paradox of the set of all men that excluded one man who did not belong to that set. It was this man that all male therapists perhaps had to aspire to, and perhaps all men ought to aspire to. But not without also being real, not without having to call themselves to account or not deny their own humanness or rather the ideologies, the language, to which they are subject and oppressed by or which they promote and may even delight in. Something they could never quite get to. I imagined she was expecting me to say I was more interested in the beauty of her mind and spirit (which by definition as a therapist I had to be). But instead I asked her what it was like to be as attractive as she was. She gave a clear answer. A burden sometimes. Men were ridiculous in how they were affected by her but also she used it to her advantage. She liked the power.

"I just have to show some curves and I get what I want" and while she said this she shifted in her chair as if subconsciously to prove the point.

Placing aside the sensuality of thoughts that crowded around me I reflexively summarised what she said about how it was a burden and that it was a way of having power over others, especially over men. She said she thought they deserved to be manipulated. But in her look was a kind of disapproval both of me and of my therapeutic speak. It seemed she did not want to meet me as a therapist employing some method or technique but rather as a person, specifically a man. She had chosen to see a man not a woman. I asked her what she thought it was like to be a man. Another marker was laid down.

"Idiotic. Aggressive. I wouldn't want to be one."

"Don't blame you," I said but she ignored my attempt at humour.

"I don't want to be a man but I want to have what some of them have. How some of them don't give a shit. And money."

I stayed silent this time. The invitation to her to continue.

"They're *all* idiotic", she smiled not unkindly holding me in her look. Repeating for me as if I hadn't heard the first time, "But they have something that I want. It's that they don't give a shit. And they have money."

I must have looked hurt (even though I thought I wasn't but actually was). One of my first ever clients once advised me never to play poker as he could read all the feelings in my eyes.

"No offence, but I'm just saying what I think is true," she said.

"None taken," I replied a little too quickly.

For a hopeless moment I wanted to show this woman how much of an exception I was. The exception to the paradoxical set. And the incongruent hopelessness of such a thought dissolved completely as the words "well, maybe a little taken" came out of my mouth of their own accord. She smiled more warmly this time.

We worked for a few months, not a long time at all. Her father had been a labourer who met a refugee in London, her mother. She was too good for him and left him. And their child also. She never saw her again but kept a photo, her mother smiling at the photographer but not quite there, withholding something as if those other non-disclosed plans were on her mind. She showed me the photo casually just like the pain in her story was interwoven casually with her telling of it. 'Have a look at this, it means nothing to me really' I imagined her saying, the weaving of casualness like the blank spaces between lines holding a message on how she coped with the world. 'Don't get too involved, people have no real value' it translated. But perhaps that was not it as there was warmth in her smile and she liked honesty. The warmth was from her father I imagined. In those blank spaces the emotional pain needed to be left alone. At least for now. The cruelty of the look of the "idiots" directed towards her in the lap dancing seemed to fit with those empty spaces too, flowing easily around her as if it wasn't there. Used to being not regarded properly as a person and not being valued highly enough from the start yet still she was warm. Maybe none of this warmth had anything to do with her father at all and was just to do with her, what she *chose* to be. Now that would be impressive. Surely she must have felt this regard in my thoughts which I felt for her even though it was not mentioned, impossible though it is to know what someone else feels unless they tell us and often even then they don't even know themselves.

In the 'transferential field' (if we want to call the relation between us that at least for a while) some of the other thoughts that crowded in were the usual ones - what kind of lover she would be and so on, which sometimes can be important in therapy but not this time. What was strange was that in the most part the phantasms in the transferential field were images of marriage of some kind, stability, and enduring love. Some of this was about possession, about owning something that was desired, about owning a person and even being owned. Although I believe in loyalty, I don't believe we should ever try to be either owning or owned, yet the fantasy like something primitive was there. It seemed to belong in the wider social world also and not just some private quirk. Why else are wedding rings and engagement rings so important to most people? They are *public* displays of belonging or ownership of a kind. The ambivalent feelings linked to such thoughts were maybe only partly my own, some maybe were hers also. I usually dismissed (a bit too quickly perhaps) any ideas of a stable emotional life linked with a stable sexual life as a fantasy. But those pictures crossing my mind were of a reality of an emotional and sexual life with another - with *her* - that was stable over time and loving. Such a thought was just a dream. Relationships at best, even the best ones, always settle into a more disappointing reality of care and perhaps flickering eroticism. Perhaps she would be happy with *that* life, that steady caring disappointment, but I doubted it. The reality of relationships becoming no longer really sexual even if still caring would be gloomy and sad for her I imagined. Such gloom was the opposite to her energy, the opposite to something about her life force that seemed to go far beyond the grasp of others. The brutal question of what she would be faced with if she were no longer attractive to someone she loved was there like a dark cloud. I wondered whether the fantasy field in this respect was all my own and nothing to do with her at all. I remained stopped on this awful horizon of disappointment. I pitied all of us as being condemned to this common tragic fate. The only way to survive was to do something fiercely creative. Something serious and not ironic so that pity is just a muddy stepping stone to something better.

In one such reverie she must have seen the brief standstill of pity on my face and mistaken it for pity for *her*. That look of hers hardened towards me. She hadn't seen the other thoughts, or that pity itself belongs in a muddy swamp of shifting meaning. "I don't pity you, I hope you don't think I do," would not be the right thing to reply to her look. One of her signposts.

"Men usually want to *own* me and you know to fuck me," as if talking about the dull weather. "I'm here because I know it won't be like that forever and I don't want it to be anyway. I won't be forever young and I have to do something different. I'm not just that. I've *already* changed. I don't need *you* to tell me how to change."

Distance and aggression were here now between us. I wondered what she needed me for then but stayed silent. Thoughts lifted and dipped in my mind like boats bobbing on water. I thought of some of those who had taught me to be a therapist. Someone had said the only way to allow women a voice that is theirs in society is to shut up. I could never quite decide on whether that was true. Maybe I should just shut up and listen. But maybe also she *did* need me to affirm something, perhaps her inner beauty in some way. It would be wrong to say "You are beautiful" even though I would have been emphasising the 'are' as if trying to convince her of that other *inner* quality of intellect she had which I was then implying she didn't see and needed to develop. And this would have been such a ridiculous thing to say. Of course she could see her inner beauty. She wasn't so distanced from herself. I was confusing my thoughts, the boats bobbing around bumping into each other getting swamped. It was me she was distancing herself from. The directness of her words nudged the thought of justifying to her something primeval in me in the name of honesty alongside that of the considerate exceptional man. It was important not to be false. Men did and *would* want to 'own' her as if she were a 'thing', a kind of ornament, just as I did at some level and she *already* knew this. Some form of cowardliness revealed itself of not being honest with myself or her. A bad faith like a rotten apple in the batch which I tried to pluck out. "I suppose we all like to own beautiful things but the problem there is the word 'thing' isn't it?" was again something I didn't say. Other thoughts in the harbour were whether or not it was only beauty that saved us, no matter how we conceived of that. Some psychoanalysts (unfortunately) call what is most desirable the phallus, not the actual phallus (although it can be mistaken for that real fleshy thing or image) but that which is most desirable in society. Indeed, here she was, the most desirable, but wanting to *have* what is most desirable also – power, money, and not to give a shit. Yet all of that stuff only held true if she had accepted what society told her what it wanted of her - if she had taken it seriously. Was that not so? Did she really want what society wanted of her? Did she know herself? She could reject it all and become a witch or something else and perhaps have a better life than society had to offer. But witches don't exist. And do any of us really have a choice? Still it could be helpful for her to know how seriously she had taken the world, how it had affected her. This would be the therapy - to get to the other side in order to laugh at it all. Thoughts seemed to stop there again. At the possibility of me knowing which direction the therapy would take. And also at the possibility of laughing at it all. Such things were like trying to know the wisdom of having lived without having lived.

I asked what it was like for her that men, or maybe everyone, wanted to own her, thinking this would help her get in touch more with her aggression. She answered with no hesitation however on the pleasure of it and its future.

"It's nice. Makes me feel powerful. Kind of cool. But the thing is I'll be forty all of a sudden and have nothing then unless I sort myself out."

"So you want to become something different before that happens?"

"Yes."

"Not to become a witch then?" I joked.

"Maybe a rich witch," she smiled.

If there is such a thing as a footnote in a conversation then this is one, regarding her smile. We all know a smile that is beautiful. Apart from the physicality, there must also be a kind of personal warmth in it, and that warmth was there, strangely for someone who could be so cynical. I couldn't help thinking that real beauty has to have a lack of vanity too and there was a lack of vanity in her warmth. Vanity it seemed to me is something to do with not admitting what we are. Phrases like, "I'm lucky to have such and such... I'm lucky to be so and so... I'm lucky to be in a situation that..." disturbed me as they often betray a bad faith. Say instead how you have pushed others aside, how you think it's yours (that you created it), or have striven for it and would never let it go and would maybe even kill for it. Be more honest about the personal violence. That is less vain at least. I wondered who I was saying that to as I listened to her. What crossed my mind showed what she wanted of me – an honesty that uncovered bad faith in oneself and others. Plans for the therapy seemed to be taking shape of their own accord but then in keeping with my philosophy I placed them aside.

I was sure she knew what I meant about being a witch - what all of feminism meant, that one alternative for a woman not to be wholly subject to men was to opt out of society's offerings and create her own reality (insofar as anyone can). No wonder there was such a market for films and TV series of teenage girls and sisterhoods of young women with supernatural powers who were forever destroying vampires and evil men, who defied exploitation and wrought justice. Although they fell in love with those men too.

As if catching something of my thoughts, a dialogue appeared between us like an apparition. She said, "Did you know that if you dress more like a teenage girl you get better tips from men in restaurants if you're a waitress? Same goes for my former work."

"I didn't know that..."

"Do you not think that's sick?"

"What it means for you is more important."

"More important than it being sick?"

"It's awful. But what you make of it personally is what is important here I mean."

"I think it's sick. It makes me feel disgusted... just confirms everything." She looked at the floor as if recalling something, the sunlight catching her profile for a moment as if she were a statue. A bank of cloud must have moved away allowing the indifferent sunlight to illuminate the room. It spread a moving pattern across the floor, the leaves from the trees outside shaping fantastic forms against the rug. Light and shade moving together in a wayward dance on the fixed geometrical patterns of the rug. We both looked at the effect, for a moment two consciousnesses focused on one point as if there were two realities moving across each other without touching and coming to agreement.

"What do *you* make of it? You must have a view," she said in a kind of tone to invoke confidences. She looked up towards me straight in the eyes. The agreement of what we had both held in view for a moment separated out again, and between us was something unknown. Her language of looking and viewing was something I held onto though. Her work had involved being viewed and now she wanted my view and the floor between us was a dance of shade and light.

"It's awful. Men who do that try to replace the law, or try to *be* the law. I suppose I'm thinking like an analyst here even though I'm not one..."

"It's all still sick don't you think? Freud was sex-obsessed wasn't he, and a cokehead?"

"It is sick about the teenage girls yes. But I'm not so sure about what you say about Freud, that's just old-"

"Old *wives* tales!" she broke in, snatching the unformed words out of my mouth. "See what you're saying!"

I felt embarrassed. It was a sexist phrase and I couldn't defend it. It took an effort not to in the same way that men often say, 'yes, but...' to criticisms from women. But I also feel some alliance with Freud and did not like him being insulted in such an unknowledgeable way. Other people who I was also fond of blatantly slandered Freud accusing him of being a cocaine addict and a paedophile and I would defend him. She was projecting something onto me however that was important to leave alone. I was not averse to talking about my own personal feelings with some clients but it didn't seem that it would be helpful to share these just then with her. It seemed she was only waiting for some defence in order to destroy a man somewhere. Or all men. I had to make a space for that. The sense of 'view' was important also. And I needed to pay attention more to what I was saying. It didn't help that my bookshelves were there with their books like scattered advertisements for psychoanalysis and then carelessly saying 'old wives' tales'.

"Yes, I see, I know," I said, hoping to acknowledge her insight but also thinking of how we are all caught up in something to do with culture and language. There is a showing and un-showing of certain aspects of one's being here. Her almost rudeness, her impatience with me. With men. She looked at me as if reading a map, noticing features perhaps that I couldn't see. But it was *her* map projected onto me (and not an objective or accurate one as none such existed). I was being 'viewed' - just as she had been - from an alien place. In suddenly being placed in her shoes to an extent, I was also placed in mine. This is one of the humilities of the therapist - that we are seen by the other often erroneously as much as we see the client, if not more. Viewed, measured. It does not mean we are understood however – that would be a mistake to assume just as it is a mistake to assume that about a client, or anyone, that we 'get' them. In therapy there is a kind of silent meeting of being most of which remains untranslatable, beyond language. Something happens due to the untranslatable. You could say the untranslatable is the 'transference' in all its forms. The client can be open to its mystery or can become disturbed by it so that they fill it in with their own creations (projections, fantasies, stories). In therapy it is better most times to allow the other person to go with their projections, stories and fantasies as part of the longer process of untying knots we get into with others. It can be painful for the therapist who has to bear it even while we still reveal aspects of ourselves all the time despite ourselves. Nothing is neat and tidy. In this instance, to get away from the discomfort of being 'viewed' I clumsily went into theory.

"Just shows you how language gets a grip on us... You know that stuff is like everything else, it's just talk, gossip, pop psychology, stuff floating about that feels like it's real," I said, trying to explain my use of 'old wives' tales'. Immediately, I regretted not staying with 'being viewed' or 'seen' as it linked so well with her former work and might open a space for her to speak of this. Still the mistake wasn't the end of the world.

"But why is rubbish the same as old wives' stuff, why not old *husbands'* tales?"

"Yes, why not?" I asked, hoping she would answer from her experience.

Throughout this exchange small expressions of consideration made it into the moving shades of no-man's land between us. Expressions that signified we might actually be able to work together. It seemed important to her that I was making a mess of this perhaps. I hoped she would see my heart was in the right place. There were other looks too. Although her expressions conveyed that she didn't want to crush me it felt like I had failed at some level that was important to her. I had driven her into theory by mistake talking about language. I was trying to spare us both pain perhaps. But I resented her for that other kind of look which said she could know anything really about me. Still for a moment I surveyed my own life and its failures from her 'view'. There were no outward signs of substantial financial success here (which she so craved). Partly my choice. It is a problem working from home, that the fantasies of the client can collapse into the signs contained in bricks and mortar. But she liked my bookshelves filled with all sorts of books and not just on psychoanalysis. She liked the expensive cherry wood cabinet. In the silence that now filled the room, which perhaps was only a few seconds but felt like minutes between us she touched the side panel of the cherry wood it seemed without noticing. It reminded me of how a child reaches out to hold its parent's hand without ever having had the experience of knowing that hand might not be there. A very early experience for her probably. Setting aside my own resentments and regrets I reached out to that hand metaphorically.

"Society does awful things to us... Look at advertising...I'm getting targeted ads about arranging my funeral..."

As she smirked at my attempt at reaching out to her there was a slight shift in the kaleidoscopic atmosphere between us. It could easily shift back or on to something else. My job was to not let her give up on the need to know herself more deeply than she had thought of, and not to give up on *herself* (even if she gave up on me). This was such a complex of understanding - what psychotherapy is about: self-acceptance in one's own fragmentation, one's own contradictions, taking responsibility for oneself and how we affect others and so much more. Even a dissolution or calling into question of what we hold dear as 'self'. I think she noticed the shift but she hadn't finished wanting to question me.

"You still haven't said what *you* think though. No offence but are you just saying what Freud or that guy Lacan would say?" She looked over the book case, picking out some titles. Her eyesight was so much better than mine to be able to read the smaller print at that distance.

She was young and I was old. The age gap between us adding to the strangeness between us.

"What did you want to know?" I asked.

"I'd like to know whether in your experience you think that all men are perverts?"

"In my experience I don't think they are, no. At least not all of them."

She waited for me to continue, for a moment reversing the roles of client-therapist. I duly continued.

"I think everyone is a blank slate when we are born and we become what we are through experiences from our early years and onwards, what we're exposed to, family, culture, and others, plus language. Some things stick with us and other things don't and some things we can change and some things we can't."

"Is there a pervert gene, do you think?"

"No, I don't think so. I don't really know though. But I think things develop due to what's happening around us as kids or maybe how we enter into language even."

"I would like to think they are not either, I mean that not all men are. I don't think my father was."

It was the beginning of spring and the starling that often took up his place in the Rowan tree in the garden at that time of year decided to announce himself just then, as if demanding silence in the room as what was about to happen was important. Perhaps he had been there all along, with his whirring calls some kind of eternal repetition but we just hadn't noticed him. The patterns on the floor seemed to be washed away by the sound and drawn by the starling we both looked at the curtain from where the song came, the shadows of the leaves from the tree outside falling across it washed out now in a fading dance of eddies and ripples from the breeze. I watched the patterns rippling across the still folds of the curtain and noticed she was focused on the curtain folds and the light on those. Her left hand dipped in and out of the folds as if trying to sort something into a particular order, arranging the folds in regular rows to get the light and the shade just right. Just when they seemed to be in order she would ruffle them again and rearrange them until she seemed satisfied. I wasn't sure whether minutes had passed as I seemed fixed to her movements and I couldn't check on the silent clock that was hidden from her view in the cabinet facing me across the room. She broke the silence eventually, looking over at me with the seriousness of an academic and straight into my eyes (as I expected now).

"This is the talking cure, isn't it?"

"Yes."

"And I'm the one who's meant to do the talking, isn't that right?"

"Yes."

She returned to the curtain folds organising and undoing the organising while something settled between us now as if in slow motion. You could say the rules of engagement were that something. I checked the clock. Maybe ten minutes had passed.

Our meetings continued for a few more weeks, with more listening and less speaking from me. She filled the space with a chain-gang of men. Paedophile men, abusive men, violent men, lecherous men, murderous men, unfaithful men, neglectful men, selfish men, addicted men, lazy men, disgusting men and useless men. There were even no good men who could not also be one or more of these. She allowed only the *possibility* of exceptions to the paradoxical set when I tried to get a little too clever in one session. Her father was one exception. What seemed to be taking form between us was that she was in the lap dancing place but not lap dancing now. She was now dressed in her casual clothes and held before her was each man who was once there, no shadows for each to hide in this time, calling each one to account. She was hiring *my* services. A stand-in. At times I felt I was harangued as if on trial personally, or sometimes the defendant or the witness, sometimes the defence but rarely allowed to be the judge, jury or prosecution. Although the therapy room was my space the space of the therapy was hers and part of my work was to hold that in place for her safely, perhaps even without her noticing. The main thing I did to signal my real role in society was to mark the end of sessions on time although she usually pre-empted those signs of power also.

When she stopped coming to our sessions without warning it caught me by surprise. She texted a message a few days later that she wouldn't be coming back and thanked me for my time. I didn't want to believe she was ending but that made no difference. I felt it would be wrong and futile to try to make her stay. She was gone. I was disturbed when she left, as if all the water had been drained from the harbour of our being together. It hit me that I knew so little about her – how she was managing for money, whether she had friends, how her father was. It felt like I was left feeling as objectified as she had felt in the world of the men she knew, examined for the possession of something worthwhile, found of some limited use, then discarded with no interest in her actual person. She must have wanted me to be a stand-in for her also, to get some idea of what that was like. But it seemed that what she most needed from me was a man to represent 'men' who she could find wanting but yet who would stay in place for her, to be called to account, to *hear* her properly so that she could be set free of something. That was what I imagined. I will never really know whether I took that place properly or whether that is what she needed. I was not her. Because she left so soon I felt I hadn't properly helped. Her view of men was so narrow that she never gave us the time to open up a more complicated sense of what men were. That not all men were abusers, that women had power. That all of us humans were 'over-written' by ideologies and endless cultural 'sense'. And all along also I wondered about her relationships with women, noticing how compassionate she was towards women, including her mother who had abandoned her. But we never got to any of that. And I was sorry we would never get to think together about the awfulness of us humans. How we dismiss each other, how we grow tired of each other, how out of no reason but an inner malice we dismiss who we perceive as the ignorant, the ugly, the no use to us, the arrogant, the threat to our narcissism, or the whoever person who just reminds us of something we are ourselves or wish we were. The sheer violence in us as human beings, the sheer potential for destruction of ourselves and the other. You don't have to look far to find it.

Her leaving so abruptly made me think of Sartre's existentialism in our freedom to choose. She chose. But at what point in our lives are we truly free to choose? You could say at what point are we liberated enough to say we are free to choose? When are we free enough to be free? Freedom then is a movement towards something. But the paradox is that one has to be free already in order to be free. This is the miraculous in therapy and life. It happens like a dream happens. Appearing like an apparition of living salvation. As this thought came to mind as if out of nowhere I felt such a relief. I was just part of her process towards freedom from her history, and she was just part of mine also. And it meant I was in a process still, a living one of miraculous happenings. We were both in a process of breaking free that seemed to me caught up in beauty when we first met but was something else altogether. I falteringly tried to summarise it in my notes. With line spacings - for space to breathe.

We were two souls crossing paths. Where space has to be opened not closed.

One in a socially sanctioned role holding a space of safety.

'Do no harm'.

The other a human being trying to *be* differently, trying to get free.

"Open the heart towards a movement of freedom," one wants to say.

"Do what you can," one can say.

Letting the other affect you and without retaliating.

Holding steady and not humiliating the other.

I mean hold that space until our own freedom kicks in, until it appears *miraculously*.

Perhaps in her leaving a freedom had appeared for her miraculously which showed her journey was elsewhere. An opening into something new (and yet I think old also). I had to accept it. And she may have left because I was not free enough to be up to the task at that time to help her further. Free of my own misconceptions. I will never know.

## Freedom that breaks through

I once had a client who spoke to me not unusually of the love of her father. There was a block with her however as she couldn't speak of feelings. Try as I might there was a kind of impossibility of feeling. I foolishly even tried to model feeling *for* her – saying how *I felt* in certain situations, tying myself in knots sometimes and becoming embarrassed. But she seemed to just absorb these examples and do nothing with them like a material absorbing all the wavelengths of light with no reflection back of anything. Although she could not speak of feeling she could speak about work projects she was doing which impassioned her. And we spoke a lot about these as a kind of habit in each session, the problems with spreadsheets, accounts, tax strategies and profits for the company until all that she had to report in each session dwindled off into those silences that are the seedbeds of learning in therapy. But nothing seemed to grow from them but awkwardness. I wondered why she continued to attend therapy, as all that seemed to be happening after her weekly 'financial report' was that I would stupidly ask a number of questions punctuating the silence that would fall around us. I felt a pressure to fill in the spaces so that something could *not* happen. Every therapist who works phenomenologically will tell you to resist this kind of pressure as much as possible and wonder where it comes from instead (although not necessarily saying that to the client). Space was something I was aware of with others and was usually good at allowing but it was difficult with her. After several months like this, not looking forward to our sessions at all I had a dream. I dreamt I was rolling around in white sheets (spreadsheets?) with a boss at work I used to have many years ago, a father figure. We were both fully clothed and the sheets tangled about us as we rolled about as if playing like a parent and child. I was clearly the child while still being an adult (young at that era in my life that the dream portrayed). The dream brought with it a sense of sensuality of the father's loving presence, benevolence and loss. I thought of my own father who I had been very close to, who I missed so much after he died, and who I missed as a child when our family went through separations. You could say it was a homoerotic dream but it felt more like a sensual dream, of the kind of embodied, sensual love that exists between a parent and a child that is always implicit and tacit but so important to ground the child in feeling loved.

The effects of this dream on the therapy was astonishing. Without having to 'do' anything, I noticed I was less inclined to share my thoughts about feelings and more relaxed, less inclined to explain and more open to sitting in the silences. She surprisingly began to speak of how she loved her *step*-father (not her father) and missed him terribly. She began to speak of the whole sensual world of their relationship when she was a child, all of which was of feeling and of being loved by him, and loving him despite his faults. The 'given' (or freely circulating, accepted) ideas of how hateful he was that circulated in her family were set aside for her own words, so she could speak of her *own* experience, rather than of what she had been taught by the 'family'. The eroticism knitted into the sensual always remained tacit, wholly sublimated, and long-overprinted by social norms, not sexualized and held safely by the boundaries of her step-father when she was a child. He was never abusive to her, and she felt safe snuggled beside him watching television, and indeed was safe as she fell asleep to him reading bed-time stories by her bed. A sense of safety and benevolence of the world that had been torn from her when the family separated and she had retreated 'into her head' to the safe world of numbers and precise calculations.

The important word here, the one that had unlocked something for us *both*, and which had given rise to my dream, was when she had said 'Dad' (not 'Step-Dad') after months of circling around something. It was not only the given sound, 'Dad', that unlocked something but also the way she said it with a profound lack of energy that flattened the sound, that indicated a sensual landscape of deadness (beneath which there is always something very much alive but oppressed and suppressed). That sound had connected with something very much alive for me which provoked my dream, which then in turn allowed her to begin to feel loved, or safe, and cared about in the room with me. You could say the sound 'Dad' (how she said it) provoked a chain of events that allowed a transference love of the father to come to life in the room. The resistance to it was also mine, not only hers. The dream connected me to my own further sense of loss of the love of the father that was unknown up to then. This is how we unfold and change, shift and move as 'selves' if we are open to that movement.

One thing we can see here from this imaginary example is that psychotherapy comprises a 'field' like a magnetic field in that both client and therapist are implicated in the work, or entangled in it in some ways that are unknown until they happen. No matter the amount of their own therapy the therapist has been through, there will always remain areas that can be changed (even though for some people some areas seem forever stationary). Extended personal therapy (at least several years' worth) of the kind that fosters openness to experience however is a preparation for responding openly to these events that happen in therapy so that we will be more free to be responsive to what goes on in the 'field'.

## On freedom in supervision

(written especially for trainee therapists in the manner of a phenomenologist, the line spacings just there to breathe. It is a fictional reverie based on real events. Not a poem.)

Dare I say I don't like reading Dostoevsky?

Or dare I say dare I say it

That I was turned on by my client?

That fantasies stretched across my mind like that Goya painting

Or worse, or worse...

Dare I say it, dare I say it,

That I was not interested in their life

But was in them.

Of course, I know,

I will withdraw my intrusive gaze,

The penetrating word

And instead become this still pool in which she may see her own reflection,

Not too limpid for her to see my depths,

Although perhaps some day yes

When all the hot-headedness has been taken out and there remains only a colder passion and big free spaces.

Then maybe you can step forward with some humour and laugh at it all.

Maybe.

This stuff is banal, the real stuff

I wouldn't dare say at all.

That was what struck me most in that research many years ago now

-

That supervisees will not say

What matters to the supervisor.

What matter.

It matters.

Just be careful not to throw your pearls to swine.
It might be better to keep it cognitive,
Or in theory,
Discuss the Real,
Or the meaning of intentionality
Or what Heidegger meant by the Nothing.
Or empty speech
I have known supervisors who keep it empty
But not many.
It is never better to keep it cognitive,
As if say what the cognitivists call groinal responses have nothing to do with the erotic landscape of the psyche
Nothing to do with them my @£$#!
But try to get that into a randomised control trial.
Primordial not even unconscious
Some desire finding its way through the body ignores the body of knowledge, all those givens, and becomes its own library of experience,
Or some desire find its way through a tangle of signifying relations, or a capillary action of the invisible.
It doesn't have to be erotegenic, or anything like that at all,
It can be the heat of an envy so surprising you wouldn't know what to say about it,
It will catch your tongue like the cat,
Such an embarrassment of passions, of jealousies and of pettiness that could become a
conflagration, a flowering,
A single mycelium suddenly flowering into a field of death caps.
Don't mention any of this in supervision for God's sake.
Jesus, god wouldn't care,
The truth will set you free.
Not always.
The body tells its lies too. Reader beware. Don't think you know.

I imagine you'll find it on your way home after supervision,

Early one morning in London,

Ordering an espresso by the river,

Noticing the so feint trace of a Caesarean scar on the drum tight skin of the waitress,

Too young surely for such a thing,

For such things,

The surgeon must have been a craftsman,

And all that eroticism changes like the colour on a bird's wing

Into something else,

Maybe sentimental,

If sentiment means feeling towards another that cannot be described

But wells up like damp,

or the iron acid water of a bog.

Am I getting this right?

Will your supervisory eyes find my scars and not make a song and dance about them?

Dare I say I don't like reading Dostoevsky?

## What are sensual relations in psychotherapy?

In order for something to change in our personal lives, or for our person, some meaning has to shift with respect to what occupies us. We all know of people for whom meaning never seems to shift however, for whom meaning just becomes more entrenched; one could say that the only change in meaning for these people is that the original meaning becomes more defined, more pronounced, and more certain. Most people are somewhere in between perhaps, where some meanings can shift but some meanings will not. The kind of meaning I am talking about here is entrenched meaning (like a cut in the landscape), that which reflects one's way of life, how one sees the world, one's relationships (past or present), how one is able to continue to 'go on', and is probably impossible to define for oneself as it is discovered as we proceed in life. But some simple examples of 'entrenched meanings' that define us can be found in the answers to problems such as what happens to meaning when we no longer love someone, or begin to hate someone; when we no longer have an 'interest' in something, a way of life, or a career, or a new interest occupies us. We may still continue to love the sunshine on a cool morning, the smell of rain in a storm, the sound of thunder, the feeling of both belonging and anonymity in crowds, relief on waking from a bad dream, but we may no longer love someone we once held most importantly in our hearts; or we are no longer interested in that friendship, that book that seemed so vital, that particular achievement that once seemed so important, and so on and on. And then, what can be more confusing, we are suddenly interested again, we had forgotten we really did like that friend, that book, that feeling of people understanding and accepting us, and so on. It is entrenched meaning that holds us together in such crises and reversals.

What creates such shifts, reversals, and revisions in meaning is another question. But I am interested here in exploring what happens in psychotherapy as a way of creating change through meaning in its entrenched sense. For example, how do I recover from loss, from tragedy, from the feeling that one is no longer important, from finitude, and how does one live knowing we all die, or from the growing certainty that one will never feel the experience of 'true love' again, or from the experience of feeling that everything one once held most precious is value-less? For example, that there is no God. From the outset, 'recovery', or a new path, happens somehow through being with another person. This is so obvious we often forget about it, that it is through the other person that we come to change, or 'become' at all. Some communication with this other has to happen for some change to occur. Often this other is framed as a lover, a partner, a 'someone' who we feel will love us 'wholly' as sexual beings. We miss out that this other can be someone who makes no personal claim on us, even a psychotherapist.

The psychotherapist is a facilitator of communication of some kind. What kind of communication? Communication through words, symbols, signs, and even 'unconscious' communication, with oneself and with others. Entrenched meaning has something to do with the private, and only has 'depth' because it is hard to see, even if it is there 'on the surface' of a dream, or in others' everyday reality of oneself. Its depth comes from its rootedness in oneself, its immanent insistence in oneself. Such depth meanings are based on sensual relations, in that what is sensual is of the experience of being embodied, or even the experience of being disembodied as embodied. We experience our lives on the simplest level and the deepest level through embodied understandings and experiences. My hands are warm, but sometimes they are not, they are cold and clammy, and this experience is related to depth meanings. I want to call them sensual meanings now as they are embodied and of memory. Like the strata of the earth, we are overlayered, interlayered, folded into, metamorphosed, faulted and even obliterated in our experiences. Out of such and in such lie the deepest of meanings that were once inherently of the senses, or sensual.

## What are given relations in psychotherapy?

Given words, expressions, ways of behaving are those that seem to have a fixed sense or meaning that we all are part of as a communicating collective. We would not be able to understand each other without knowing about these 'given' signs. For example, when I say to you I need a new pair of shoes, you generally will know what I mean. The sound 'shoe' links with a rough concept of 'something to put on your feet for walking about'. We won't try to pin down exactly for now what 'shoe' means or could also mean (for example, the sound 'shoo' as in to 'shoo away' can be distinguished from 'shoe' only in the context of its utterance), although it is clear there is already a network of possible other meanings. When it comes to psychotherapy and the intuitively helpful idea of understanding another's meaning, it seems that transparency of understanding is a good thing. And it can be *sometimes*. But 'given' signs tend to draw on a well of traditional or culturally in vogue meanings within contexts that are assumed to make sense, so that even without knowing it we are jumping to conclusions or immersed in something we are unaware of when we repeat one of these 'uses' of meaning.

Diagnostic categories are a good example. For example, a young nurse I knew was once verbally attacked by her mentor for not recognising post-natal depression: They had been on a visit to a woman with a new baby, and while her partner looked on helplessly the new mother cried and cried uncontrollably. The young nurse was unable to get across that it may have been that the new mother had suddenly realised she never wanted a baby, or never wanted her partner, and so it was more about a realisation of a tragedy than the post-natal depressive episode triggered by chemical imbalances which the mentor was trying to convey. The mentor's view here is guided by 'given' signs that translate into meanings that form a convention in medicine (taken for granted, as if they are 'natural'); whereas the nurse was thinking of more private, individual, or what I have called, 'sensual' meanings belonging to the subject's (the new mother) own set of signs (even though this set of signs is always part of or drawn from the wider field of language). Both the mentor and the young nurse could be right in terms of what is affecting the mother, but what is crucial is that *both* sets of signs are allowed recognition. The sensual meanings in this example were overruled, however, by the given signs of the mentor, who expressed her power quite violently (and stupidly). In almost every case, the given sign is often just a signpost towards the sensual signs, but if the given is taken as the 'true' meaning then the whole sensual field of signs is ignored along with the subject's experience. This clearly has implications for psychotherapies. Another aspect of this is that the young nurse will be *imagining* what might be going on for the new mother, but has not actually asked her to speak about what is going on. So, the sensual signs the young nurse is imagining are always *her own* signs, coming from her own imagination and may have nothing to do at all with the young mother's experience. So, it is the other person's words that are most important (the young mother's), and our own understanding of those are not necessarily of any help. It is the young mother's understanding that will bring her relief, and that may or may not include the given understanding of her experience.

Another example is the experience of listening to a couple or a group speaking in a language you do not understand. There is an easy flow of what always seems like rapid, nonsensical noises, slowing at times, pausing, stopping, and eruptions of laughter, smiles, responses of touch that show us there is something sensual happening. The whole sensuality of the other person is being touched by these 'random noises' of language strung together in a logic we do not understand because it is foreign to us. Such noises are called 'signifiers' by linguists. They are the stuff of psychotherapy if we think of therapy in a psychoanalytical sense but also as having something to do with speaking, and also if we think of it in terms of simple sensual relations. For the latter (the sensual relations of the other person) this indicates the need for therapy as an elucidation of the *other person's sensual signs*, the whole network of private meanings in which they will have been, and continue to be, immersed. If we meet the other person with given signs, we are just imposing or repeating accepted meanings upon them, or distorting their spoken words into our own conventions or unexamined ideas. We have to instead pay close attention to the sensual signs that the other person speaks as these lead us into a world that is not ours, but more crucially helps the other person find the strange world that is theirs. Unless the other person is seriously deranged, they will be able to find and make sense of their own world.

## The sensual and the given are always together

Learning often comes spontaneously in the moment in therapy, in the unusual spaces and atmosphere of therapy as talking, thinking and being together with another. How the learning happened then disappears like a dream. It is hard to 'capture' in the moment - perhaps impossible. It comes in response to an environment, in a dialogue with the client as if by magic and then is so difficult or impossible to recount later on. But those moments may not occur if the therapist has not been through something of a 'formation', a hard struggle with others - including the others with whom he has engaged over a lifetime of living - and a hard struggle with himself. Psychotherapy is not a technique then that one learns - although there are ideas that are technical (theoretical in a sense) that others have formulated as in any thought-through practise. What drives the struggle so that it doesn't end in bitterness is love, love for one's own therapist, one's peers and colleagues, one's teachers (or lecturers more often than not). Or what can drive this process even may be what is mistaken for love yet has the same effects. That doesn't mean one has to love everyone involved, of course.

If I have an agenda in therapy it is for the other person to come to know themselves, and yet most of what I have learned, or what emerges, comes from the effects of the client on *me*. The client has helped me to know myself in relation and what I have learned is often uncomfortable, challenging an idea I had of myself. But it is not often that uncomfortable, as the value in the revelation outweighs the discomfort of knowing. And the value is *returned* to the client hopefully with a dividend or a windfall of new understanding.

The same happens in similar life situations, in supervision, in one's own therapy, or unusual conversations with people. I am trying here also to catch some of the learning as it was in those moments just before the 'how' and the 'what' of it disappeared and still leaves us changed, even though we cannot often recall what happened, or what we recall is a rationalisation of something else. The idea of the sensual isn't new, but it appeared new to me when I discovered it for myself. This is what we all need to do – discover through experience. What I noticed later on was that whenever something seems to happen that is therapeutic, or is calling out to be so, there is a sensual experience happening also.

Whatever emerges through this process has an unusual value to me, and I'm not definitely sure if this value translates into having value for *others* every time. In therapy I think yes. It comes out in different ways, sometimes through painstaking thinking over and over again on what I feel or experience until I can say, "yes, that's like it, that's like it enough." And sometimes it comes out in simple thoughts straightforwardly found, also in those 'disappearing moments' of therapy. And so all of it is a recollection in progress that is also an invention.

How to think of a sensual meaning then? Things reverberate across time, what we think of as the past, but also in the present – changing as they do so in each moment, so that meaning and our experience of meaning transforms. I want to change this word reverberate to a made up one, 'verberate', to indicate something about the action of words upon us. When things do not transform, or if they change temporarily and then return to what they were, we get a sense that there is a 'structure' here – like the arrangement of atoms in a molecule that is very 'stable'. Sometimes the instability of something becomes the marker of its stability or form.

I imagine *'verberations'* as something like the way pebbles thrown into a pond send waves into each other in every direction and then that pond itself becomes a pebble dropped into an ocean, but if you think of all of this in three or four dimensions. We can only catch glimpses of what is going on in being - if we think of a glimpse as any way of apprehension. At the moment there is a small spider abseiling from a point on a seven-pointed pale green leaf on the ornamental maple beside me in its large orange pot. The spider is a speck amongst the jungle of leaves yet it shows an intentional organisation that is more marvellous than the huge plane that has just passed over low down sending a backwash of pressure waves crashing across the rooves of the houses as if they are ocean waves washing over a reef. This experience of being in the waves while noticing something else is what I mean by the sensual. Or begin to mean. Because I don't know what it means either fully. We are immersed in it but often miss it by thinking too much, or by thinking too little. We couldn't notice it all. Two blue bottles in a zig-zag dance like smoke particles being hit by molecules in the air move erratically (Brownian motion) but also like jaywalkers crossing roads and buzz so loudly – more loudly than the plane, past the colours on my hat. I don't need to watch them to recall the shimmering glassy blue of their abdomens, the delicate wings and legs, and the repulsive alien mouthparts. They both attract and disgust at the same time but I would never crush one as I used to do as a child - the cruelty of children is also part of the sensual – but never say never. A saintly man once told me he went through a phase of burning ant's nests as a child. His current saintliness wasn't some 'reaction formation' to sadism, but rather just thoughtfulness and that the conditions that provoked the aggression had dissolved. Another saintly man however continued with a version of his childhood cruelty by becoming a teacher (and priest) humiliating children in the classroom, as it was just something he enjoyed too much to give up.

The sensual has a similar relation to sexuality as the colour orange has to the whole electromagnetic field of which the rainbow is just the visible. If some therapist's vagina is twitching, or some other therapist's erogenous zones are making themselves known in some way, then although those 'verberations' reverberate into the spectra of the sensual ocean they are still the colour orange, even if driven through mysteries and the mucilaginous web of signifying relations, memories, images, scents and sense. What I mean is that they are not the whole picture. Not that anyone can grasp the whole picture. In this way the body can lie as we may read something into its responses that is not true.

Engorging body tissue may not have anything to do with what you may think or experience before you, and although it likely emerges from a 'significance', a meaning, this may not be that easy to get to, or you may not get to it at all.

When we begin to try to express the sensual - try to make 'sense' of it - we fall into 'given' ways of expressing something, as if we are trying to squeeze our bodies into off-the-peg clothes that just don't fit and never will. The whole world becomes a distraction of trying to explain something that cannot be explained. Trying to fit something that never fits. I really mean 'the whole world' here – that world of humans. It is the cause of the greatest distress and mindless actions. Studying history can help show this. Trying to be satisfied with an explanation so we can move on and forget about things – always, and often too to forget our own savagery, another aspect of the sensual.

It is difficult sometimes to get any sense of the sensual of someone else. We run from it because something about them disgusts us, or something about them reminds us in ourselves of something we don't want to know about – not necessarily the same thing. Where and how do you talk about something that disgusts you in relation to someone you are meant to feel empathy for, say, for example, even if you love someone? Or if they're your client?

In the sensual we experience something that given words fall short of, or compress, or dilute, and we are trying to express something which at first we may only dimly perceive but also may never come to understand or properly conceive.

## Cruelty

It is so important that children are allowed to speak, or to express themselves fully in some way, and without fear. Yet fear too is important to stop them creating their own perverse laws. You've heard of *The Lord of the Flies*. The cruelty in humans is shown more obviously in the cruelty of children. In the ants' nests client (above) there was clear differentiation of the motivation for the aggression. He gave up on the cruelty when he just found within himself a sadness and disgust at harming the insects one day – something in him had already been placed there or found there, which disturbed his cruelty as if from below so its foundation was permanently disrupted. This client linked his phase of cruelty to a major disruption in his childhood when during his parents' divorce they tried to make him choose sides. He would rather burn the house down.

Another client however, enjoyed harming animals so much that she graduated on to cruelty to larger animals, namely humans. She carefully avoided overt cruelty to humans however, as they were less defenceless, but became a lover of regulations and rules in organisations. These delimited her zone of operations in cruelty to others, but more importantly widened that zone as the regulations were full of loopholes which she exploited mercilessly. The regulations also gave her a safe space to hide in, so she could function as if she were a decent human being. She came to therapy because she wanted to develop her interpersonal skills as someone had made a complaint about her at work that she lacked empathy. She was sent on an in-house course to learn about empathy and did very well (top of the class) but thought she would go one better and see a therapist. She didn't last long as she saw nothing wrong in how she related to others. She left soon after beginning since her logic was that I didn't offer the kind of therapy she was looking for which was to help her become more empathic but (without her knowing this) *remain the same*.

## Innocence

Things we say and do in therapy reverberate across time, our bodies, souls, minds and more - what I mean by 'more' is that there are ways of being that evade words that perhaps only the best poets, writers, musicians, mathematicians, physicists, and artists even come close to showing - but perhaps any innocent can match with a look or in the momentum of being. What is an innocent? Someone who hasn't been polluted by a certain kind of education? That is, someone who can act on what they see or hear; someone who is not disturbed by conscience...? No, not that.

Is innocence not the annoying lack of understanding of the malice in others? Or in oneself?

Innocence then is not something that lasts too long in therapy, unless it is part of the fabric of the psyche to such an extent that it would do harm to unravel it. The therapist makes a judgement here.

## Just in time

The urge to care has many sources. One source is anger. A young woman once came to see me after having been at a friend's wedding. She had been there with her partner, a man her own age. They were part of a larger group of young friends and they had all known each other for several years. Extricating herself from the lively wedding dance hall she had found herself sitting with an upset old woman in the hotel lobby listening to her life story. The old woman wasn't part of the wedding group. She even inexplicably put her arm around the woman, something she wouldn't have usually done even with a friend. Her partner remained in the dance hall and did not seem interested that she was sitting with this stranger in the lobby. She left the wedding soon after and made her own way to bed. Her partner did check on her out of politeness but immediately returned to the party.

She told me how she couldn't forgive him for an affair he had while working away for six weeks. This was before the advent of mobile phones or the internet, and they had only been able to stay in touch through letters and occasional phone calls. On his return, they met up again on the day of her graduation. In her flat that morning they had "made love" (her words) together. She felt it necessary to say that she felt so profoundly loved that morning and also sexual that her body shocked her.

"It was more than just sex. It was like we were just warmth like we just were lost in each other and it had to be that way we were no longer two people but just one." She looked at me confused, a little embarrassed.

"Just speak. It's okay" is what I wanted to say and can't recall whether I did say that. I'm not sure what happens in these moments in therapy but it seems there is something human that shows itself in the room or in some other way, perhaps in the face or expression of each person that is a communication of trust which makes the other feel safe. From the therapist there must be a communication of a kind of total lack of thinking of oneself as being 'above' another, and much more of a companion in humanness that conveys something like 'I have been there too, in places *like* this, although your experience is different to mine and you are not me'. After split seconds of the pause she continued speaking in a stream of consciousness "something really wild in me that wanted to have sex, just sex and love love and sex not separated and I really wanted to be *pregnant*. I'd never been you know I mean it I'd never been so sexual it wasn't embarrassing I didn't care I just wanted him it felt like we were one..." and here she faltered, "and that one-ness was to create another one, you know."

It seemed important then it felt that I was a man as she was declaring something about herself that needed to be heard for her, or to be recognised for her; that a man needed to be *for* her in this moment - and not for himself - of describing her experience. There is a kind of love in this being *for* the other person, and it easily becomes folded into sexuality because of that sense of 'one-ness' it conveys. It is up to the therapist to shelter the other from any confusion or danger here.

She continued. As they lay tired on their bed, her partner had spoken about how beautiful she was, and she spoke too having forgotten how beautiful he was and how his body seemed especially to be made for hers, and hers for his. She described his body, and what he liked about her body, what she liked about his body too, as if they were sceneries that ought to be preserved in a piece of art. In some sense it felt like I was the canvas for a while for her to remember by, and I had become part of the scene yet separate. This separateness while also a 'wit(h)ness' was important in order for what was happening between us to be therapy. We could not 'merge as if our experience was 'one' with mine as that would destroy what she needed from me.

But almost immediately after they had had sex, he confessed about the unfaithfulness to her when he was away - with the same woman for a few weeks; an older woman, he insisted, "nothing like you, not a patch on you". She described slowly how she reacted as if she were a stranger to herself, like she had stepped out of the scene and time had slowed. She felt a chill, and pulled the duvet closer around her, all the heat and one-ness disappearing into feelings of being alone. She picked at the wallpaper where it was frayed. Her throat felt like the dry plater behind it. She said very little, she couldn't recall, or nothing at all, and he spoke a lot, she couldn't recall what. Something about it meaning nothing repeatedly. He could be very convincing. Her graduation was in a few hours. It was her PhD. Could he not have waited to tell her later? - she didn't say that to him. But that is what she said in the room with me, amongst an ice storm of other things; as if that detail of telling her *before* the graduation signified something even worse than the affair. There is a photo of the graduation. Everyone looks so pleased, even her partner, except for her, her face showing a disappointment that must have seemed odd to others that day. Perhaps they thought she was overwhelmed. She showed me the photo. Apart from the disappointment there was also well-disguised anger in her face she could see now.

"Why did I suddenly, well not so suddenly maybe, start caring for others so much soon after this, like putting my arm around the old woman a few months later? Why did I not do something different?"

A heavy silence filled the room just like clouds can overshadow a landscape until words began to fall from the silence like a relieving rain.

"Caring and not caring," she almost whispers as if thinking aloud.

"You cared about something, and didn't care about something else?" I say more loudly.

"Yes. I cared about others suddenly and didn't care about myself suddenly, I think," she lifts her voice in tune with mine.

"A regression to something maybe...? I mean going back to an earlier way of being as a child maybe..."

"To not caring about myself, like?"

"Yes, maybe, and to caring about others or another instead..."

It's hard to capture the significance of silences here but a silence followed that may not have lasted more than a few seconds but in that space of time it seemed millions of seconds of time passed in thought that illuminated her even as she looked away from me towards her hands on her lap.

"Oh dear God", she falls back to a whisper. "What the fuck is wrong with me?" knowing all too well what it was.

"You let people you love shut you up," I said for her. It may not have been necessary to say anything but I said it to acknowledge an understanding that was just there between us.

A different silence entered the room this time that seemed to want to stay like a long lost friend. Seconds stretched out into minutes. The scenes she had described played out in my mind like a wordless Chinese shadow theatre unravelling a story. I couldn't really know what her story was. I could only imagine what was going on in her mind but I knew she was *here* and that was where she needed to be, just in time even to save her life perhaps. Out of the theatre shadows a translation into words might be 'Or you can't show your anger with people you love, or wish loved you, or who remind you of someone you wished loved you, or you once loved'. My job was to not let her go until she had put her own words, colours and substance to those shadows. I had to actively 'get in the way' as it were to prevent a self-destructive tendency taking hold that would be disguised as 'care for the other.'

## The red hat society

We want a person who is only 'for me'. In the anonymous crowd of humanity, in the committees and lonely meetings to do with organisations, profit, knowledge, or achievement in the world, we still want that which is only for me. And we lose sight of how 'that which' is of course always a 'who', a person, another human being. It is as if this 'own-liness' is an ontological necessity. But it is an 'as if' – I mean it isn't really ontologically necessary.

We find substitutes for it in a relation to God, sometimes a mystical god and not so much a religious one. Or substitutes in a child, which is always wrong. Or pale substitutes in an animal or a love of plants or the natural world.

But what we have to draw attention to is the *necessity* of such a person who is 'for me' in the first place. Does such a necessity really exist? Is it just a cultural imposition of some kind? A collective delusion?

And what of its obverse, that we need someone to be there 'for'?

We take the first case so much for granted that it feels 'natural'. And have to think a little more to consider the second case - being there for someone - as 'natural'.

The weight of the impulse that pushes us towards needing 'one other' just for us, only for me, pushes us to stop thinking about it. The weight, the heaviness of it, gives us the impression that such a relation needs to be fulfilled before a sense of wellbeing can ever be restored in the psyche. The impression is that of a 'without this' you can be nothing. We can sense here the despair of the human being because even if one 'has it' nothing is really changed and that is unfortunately or fortunately true. The fortunate/unfortunate is an undecidable here. But I wish that others who I love will never know this and will stay and settle on the 'having', on the decidable that seems natural. I wouldn't want them to have such despairing knowledge of the undecidability of it.

But still can we go beyond such a knowledge? So that we can take undecidability out of the equation altogether. Can we walk *through* such knowledge as if it were a thick fog to find a 'beyond' of it? A beyond that is not about the invention or hope of some god, but is about being human?

Is immersion in the animal world, or immersion in the world of exchange relations, or the world of traditions enough? It seems like it has to be, seems natural that it has to be. But there are so many doubts.

One problem is that some of us are born to *travel*. Or we have been impelled into that course through early collisions (you might say) and no opposing force has brought us to a stop. And so we won't be satisfied with the animal world (of being a person of nature), with exchange relations (of being a person of commodity exchange both in material and mental goods), or with tradition (of following how it has always been in rituals and social practice) although those ways are always there, repeating inexorably like gravitational laws. Those ways are not immoral. Although they can be. For the traveller it is difficult to find a reason to live but find one she must. This is our work. We have to find a way to live in life's absurdity.

Let's propose an hypothesis. Let's imagine a world where one only feels worth anything if one possesses a red hat. But to get a red hat you have to have a wife (read partner/husband as you need to) who stays with you for at least ten years although preferably for life. You can then after ten years be presented with a red hat. And likewise the partner can too. You will have to have passed through certain trials however to get the hat. You will have to have lived together in the same house for most of the time, gone on holidays together, and shared a life together in the most ordinary ways and this will have to be documented and confirmed by the relevant authorities. Having children can be helpful to your cause but not essential. Once you get your hat then you will be fulfilled in the eyes of good society. You will have led and be capable of leading a good life. You will be able to make executive decisions about others who also aspire to having a red hat. What is essential is that all of this is unspoken, deniable, refutable, with no actual institutions to promote its continuity or enforcement. Nothing is written about it, nothing prescribed or proscribed in law about it, nothing compulsory or regulated about it. In fact, there is a complete openness to other coloured hats, or no hats at all. But nevertheless everyone wants a red hat and does not feel fulfilled or acceptable to society and indeed even to themselves without one. This is what we are up against when we say we want to face life's absurdity and be free of it.

## Looking out

When we look out it seems we are looking through the clearest of windows into a world that is out there and not in here. This is the experience of seeing, looking, receiving the outside through vision. But it is more than vision because it seems we are looking at a whole world of action and other beings which we move around amongst but are never part of or joined up with. We are aware we are moving around and participating amongst others but we are not in a one-ness with the outside. I may even be lost, having forgotten myself, in some conversation or activity, say cooking, with someone but still I am separate in my separateness.

Even in the experience of forgetfulness when we feel we are part of something, wholly involved, it only takes a small shift to dislodge us back into looking through windows. Take romantic love, for example. The phenomenon of it seems to throw a unity of feeling and experience around the two in love, as if the two are one. The two moving around in the everyday can in moments of one-ness feel as if the outside world is a blur of colour, vivid scenes and scents, even traffic noise is blurred, music, the laughter and sounds of others, but nothing impinges on this one-ness as it blurs out the outside. It is as if we two are one looking out at the whole sensual world through the blurred lights of rain on city window panes. We are moving around and protected from it all. But even from such a one-ness we are expelled, by certain jolts unique yet ubiquitous, such as a jarring word or a physical pain, or anything that indicates 'something beyond us', an awkward look, a hesitation, or slightly too long a silence.

While we are wholly dependent on the world (and the world of others) we are also wholly separate from both and this is our anxiety-inducing gift as humans. A gift to each of us from fate, contingency or chance. We secretly wish for one-ness with the other, with anything that promises the welcome of belonging, with a god, with a group, with a person, to remove ourselves from the anxiety of such separation. But it is better to embrace it, isn't it? I am both with and without you (singular and plural) at the same time.

### The self as an idea to be continued

There is a legal self, and therefore a criminal self. As a self you become a citizen of a society whose laws you have to respect.

There is a physical self (the living body). But there is no self that is psychological. There is only the phenomenological self. And this is why we can change.

We have to address psychosis. This is the phenomenological self at its barest. That has not yet settled into an idea of itself.

The problem with categories such as we find in diagnostic manuals is that they are written as if these categories are ontological. The matter is already settled but the self is far from it.

From experience the problem remains of how psychosis settles into an idea that is stable.

There is also the other problem of psychopathy - the extreme indifference to the other here before us. This seems to be an idea of the self that has settled for good.

The phenomenological self must be just a fire of ideas.

To be continued.

## About the Author

Anthony (Tony) works in private practise as an existential-analytical psychotherapist. His interests range all over the place from art and philosophy to gardening. And then there are the strange marvels that consciousness and life are, and in that we are here at all.

Read more at www.speakingforyourself.co.uk.